How to Draw Trucks Books for Kids (A How to Draw Trucks Book for Kids With Advice on How to Draw 39 Different Types of Trucks)

This How to Draw Book Uses a Step by Step Approach to Show Kids How to Draw Cement Trucks, Garbage Trucks, Lorries and Many Other Kinds of Trucks

HOW TO DRAW TRUCKS

Introduction for Parents

Drawing is an essential part of a child's development, stimulating parts of the brain that are responsible for creative thinking and imagination. From a young age, we are all creatively encouraged to draw, whether it be at home or pre-school. Drawing is often encouraged to improve our fine motor skills and hand-eye co-ordination; this co-ordination is vital for future academic success and for improving our penmanship/handwriting skills.

From toddler's 'scribbles' to more refined 'matchstick men' and recognisable shapes, you may find that as your child grows they will want to tackle a more complex way of drawing (perhaps it's an image they have seen in a book) but as they begin to put pencil to paper they may have no idea where to start, causing frustration and annoyance.

With the help of our 'How to Draw' book series, this frustration will disappear as we guide your child step by step, line by line, to create their very own masterpiece!

Each illustration is deconstructed and simplified into lines and shapes which will not overwhelm your child. As we guide them to form each simple line and shape together on the paper, the image gradually becomes more detailed, textured and visually appealing. Practice will always make perfect, so encouraging your child to repeat the initial steps will incite a sense of self assurance that they are able to improve their skill line by line.

If Your Child Struggles With This Book

The rate of cognitive development varies from child to child and, as such, where one child may be ready for this book another will not. If you feel that your child is not ready for this book at the moment, take it away and bring it back to them in six to twelve months.

If your child is not ready to draw step-by-step, he or she may prefer to work using grids. Grid drawing involves copying information from one grid to another using coordinates. The type of copying required in grid drawing is very useful for the brain as, in particular, it exercises working memory. Working memory involves holding onto information temporarily and then using that temporarily held information at the same time. Working memory is an important process required in maintaining attention and exercising it will be beneficial for a range of activities, including in class at school.

Dr James Manning
Consultant Clinical Psychologist

HOW TO DRAW TRUCKS

Here are all of the drawings in this book. I guess it must seem like there is a lot of them when they are looked at all at once!

Luckily, I am not going to ask you to draw them all straight away. The best way to learn to draw is one step at a time. Each drawing in this book may require between 50 and 100 strokes of your pencil, but all you will need to think about is drawing one stroke at a time.

As you use your pencil, stroke by stroke, working your way through this book, you will eventually be able to create all of the drawings!

Drawing Step-by-Step

Now I have shown you the basics, if you follow the rest of this book I will show you how to create 39 different drawings step by step. Each step will build on the previous one until eventually you have 39 complete drawings.

To make things easier for you, please download the outline grids for the drawings. You can download this additional book with all of them inside for free by visiting the web address below:

https://www.lipdf.com/product/trucks/

At first, you find my step-by-step approach too complicated or difficult please leave it to one side and come back to it later. Instead, you may want to use an alternative grid with numbers and letters on it first. By following the coordinates and matching them up with the coordinates on a blank grid you can redraw the pictures this way instead.

I have put details below about where you can download these basic grids for free on the internet.

https://www.lipdf.com/product/grids/

You can of course ask an adult to help you draw the grids instead, or you may even feel able to draw them yourself.

1. Drawing a basic grid outline will help you to give your picture good proportions.

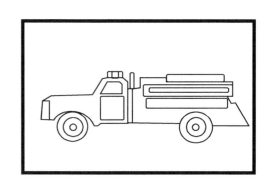

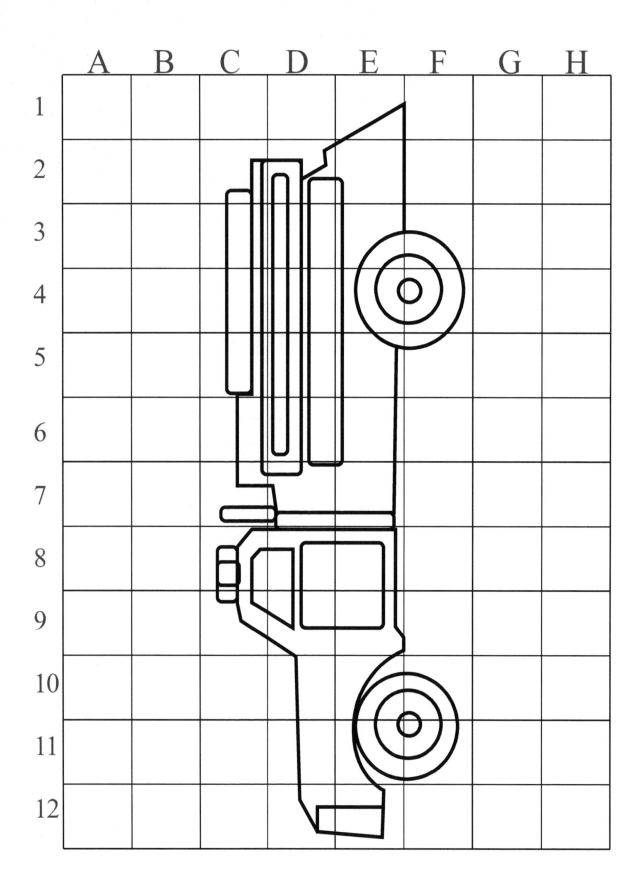

2. You can develop the direction your drawing takes with the use of a few carefully positioned lines on your grid.

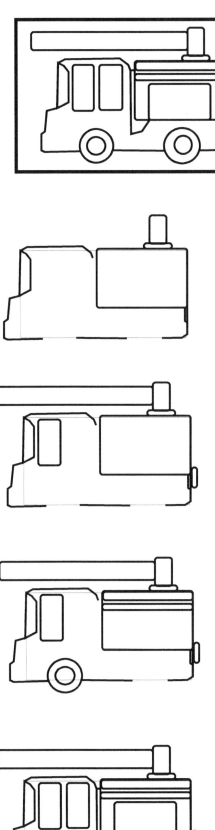

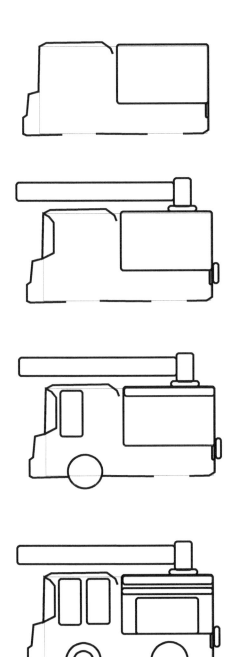

	A	B	C	D	E	F	G	H
1								
2								
3								
4								
5								
6								
7								
8								
9								
10								
11								
12								

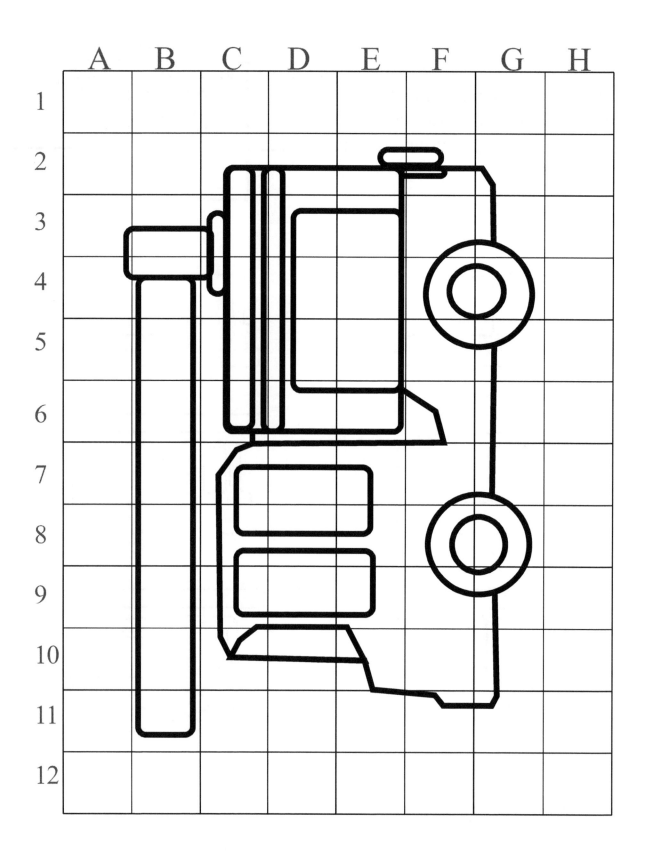

3. Separate your grid into sections to help you decide how you want to proportion your drawing.

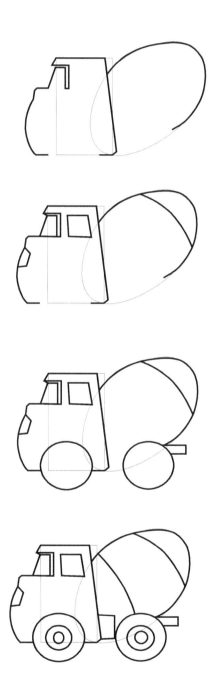

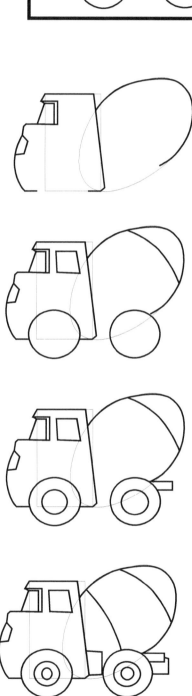

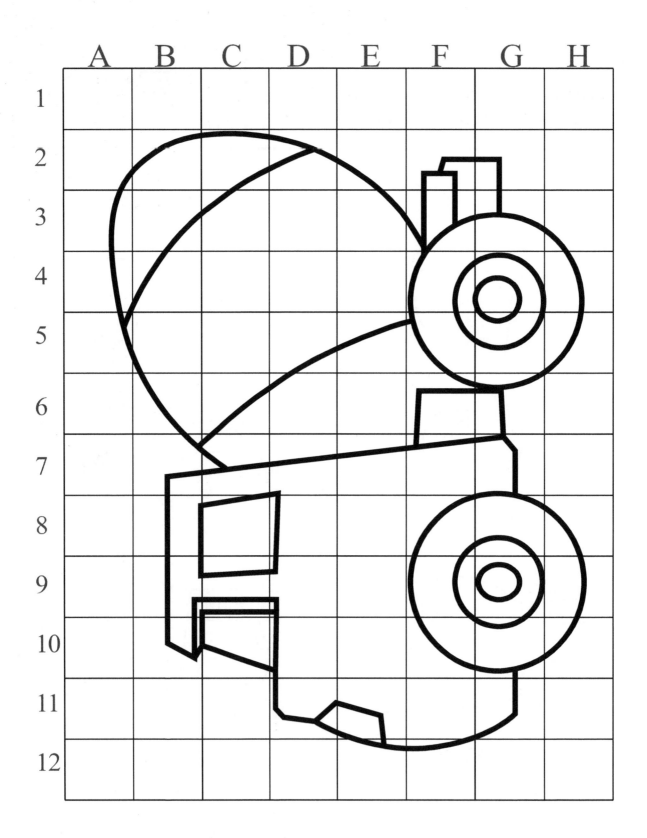

4. Sometimes starting with an outline of your drawing can be very helpful.

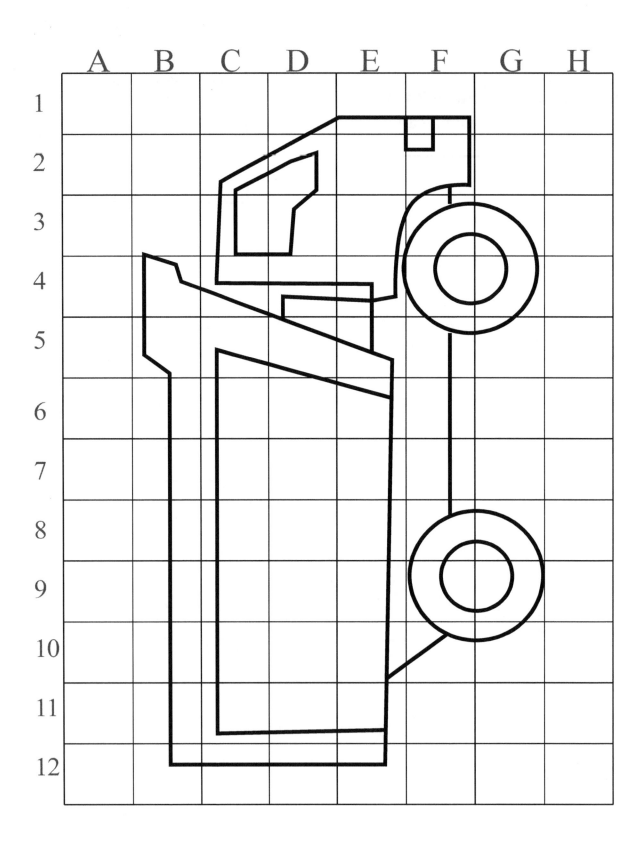

5. Drawing a basic grid outline will help you to give your picture good proportions.

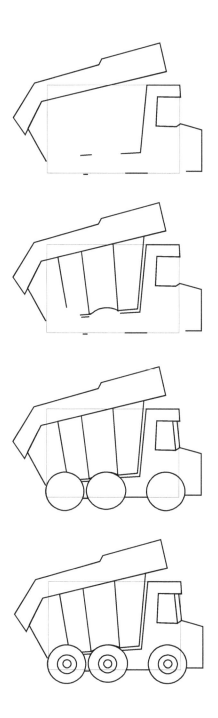

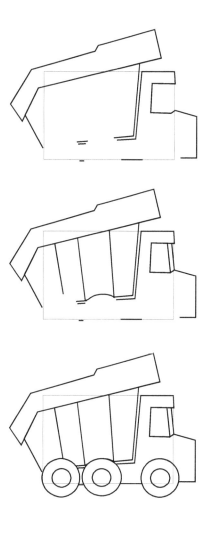

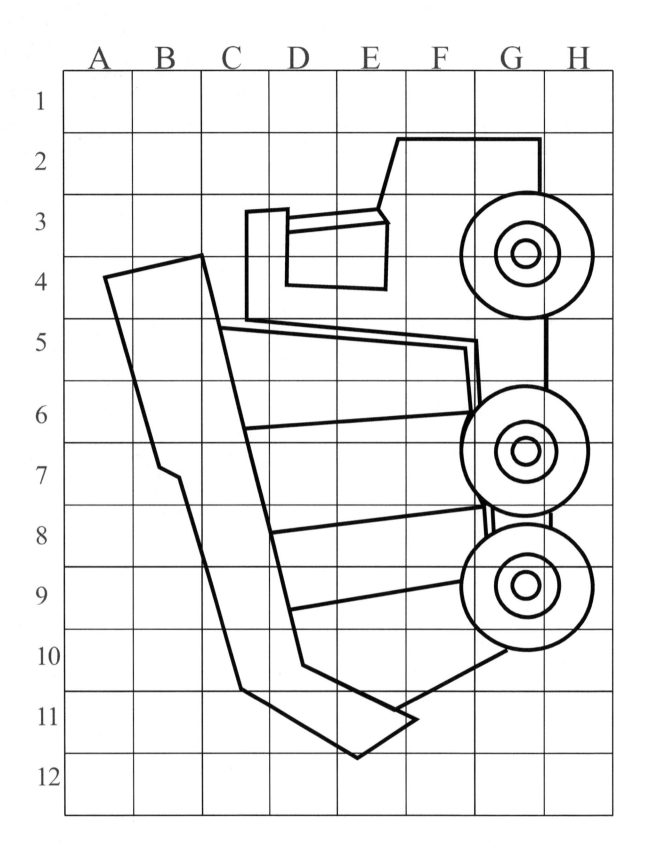

6. When starting a more complex drawing it is best to think of it as a lot of small parts. Focusing on one small part at a time will make your project feel less overwhelming.

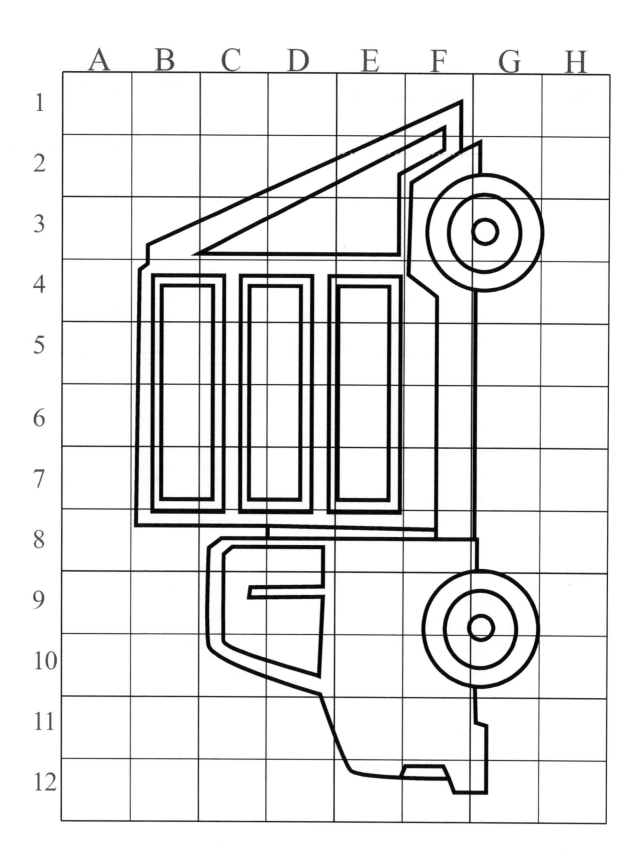

7. Adjusting the pressure you place on your pencil will help you vary the thickness of your lines.

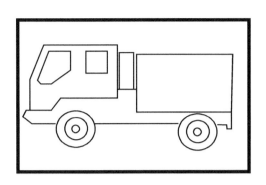

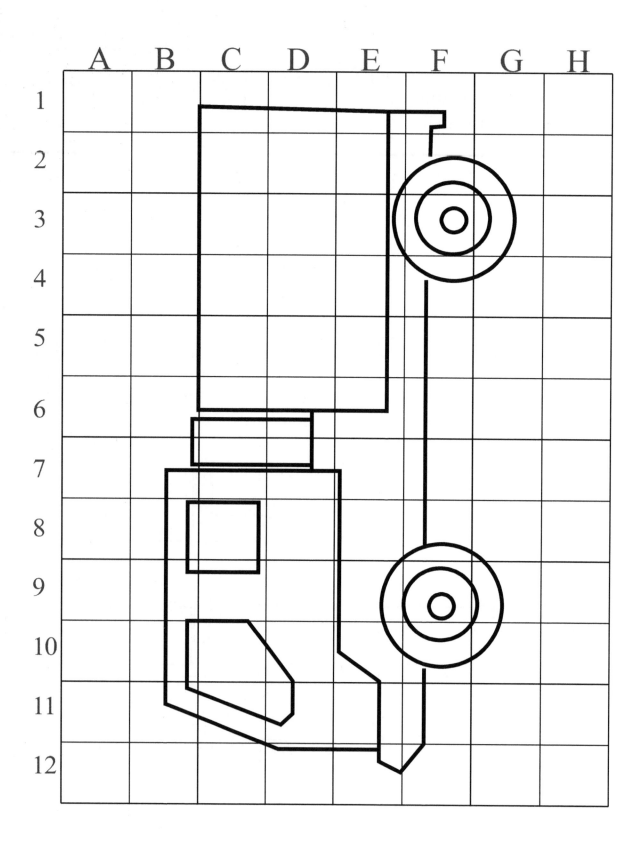

8. There is no right way to draw a grid. It is a simple rough outline to get you started.

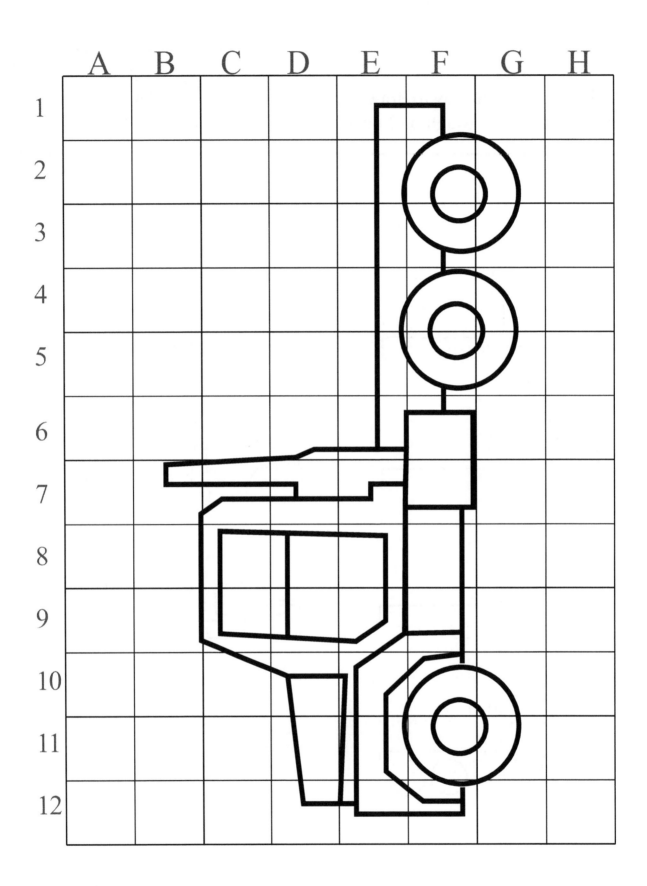

9. You can make your drawing more original by exaggerating some of its features.

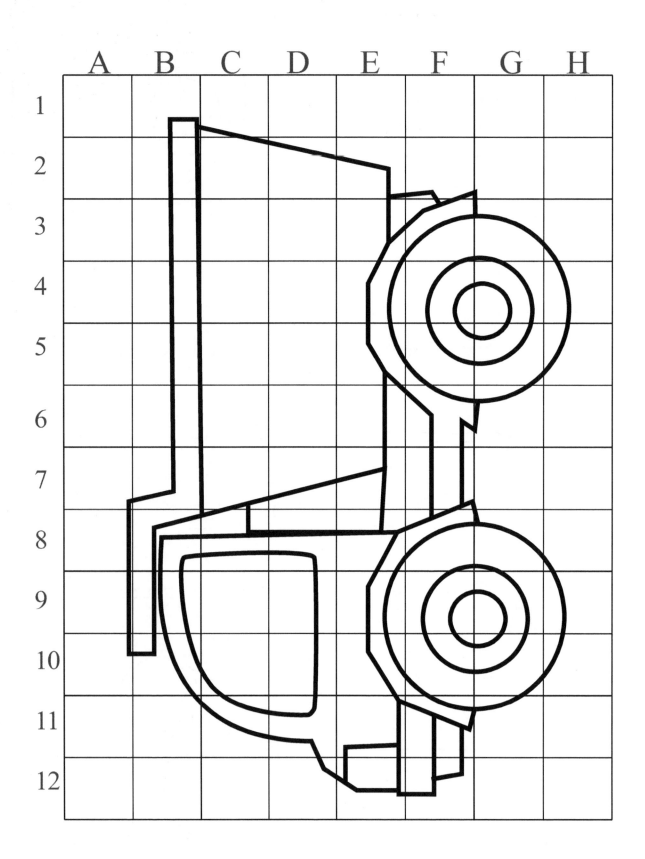

10. Try enlarging different parts of your drawings to create different effects.

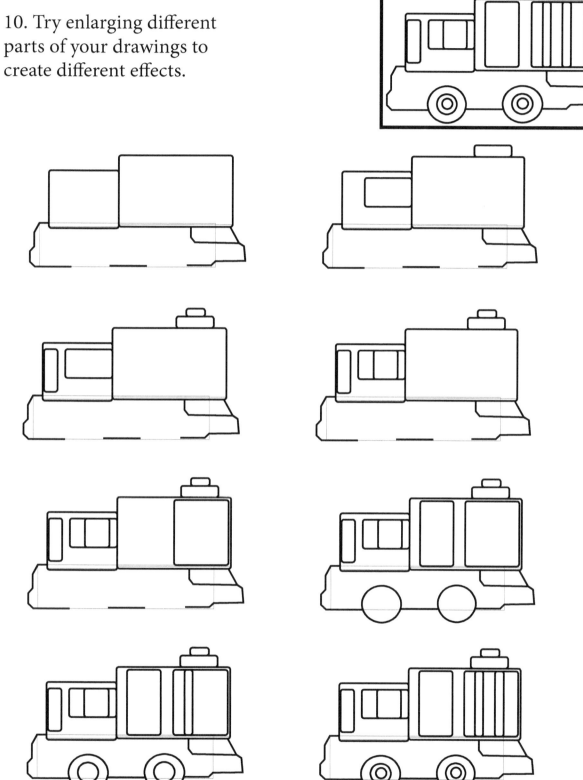

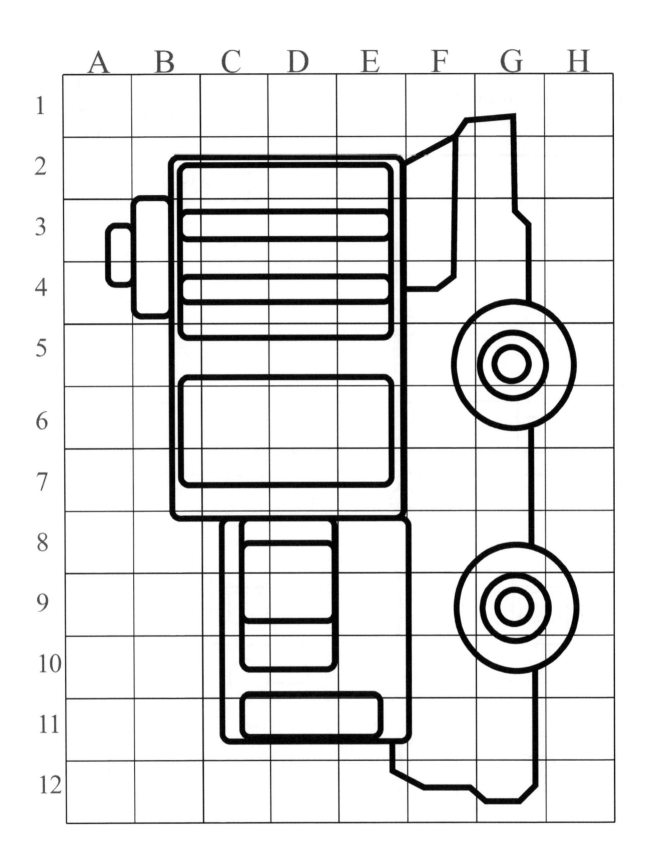

11. Try altering your
drawing slightly to create
a different look.

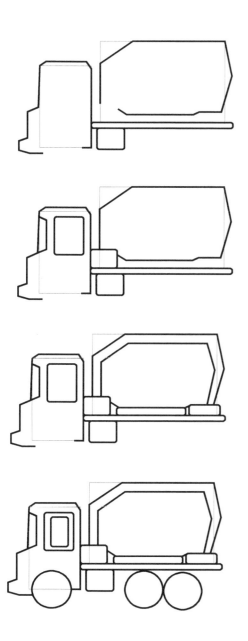

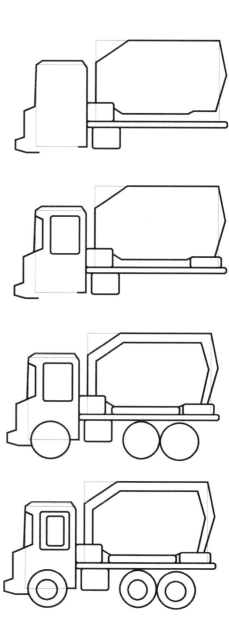

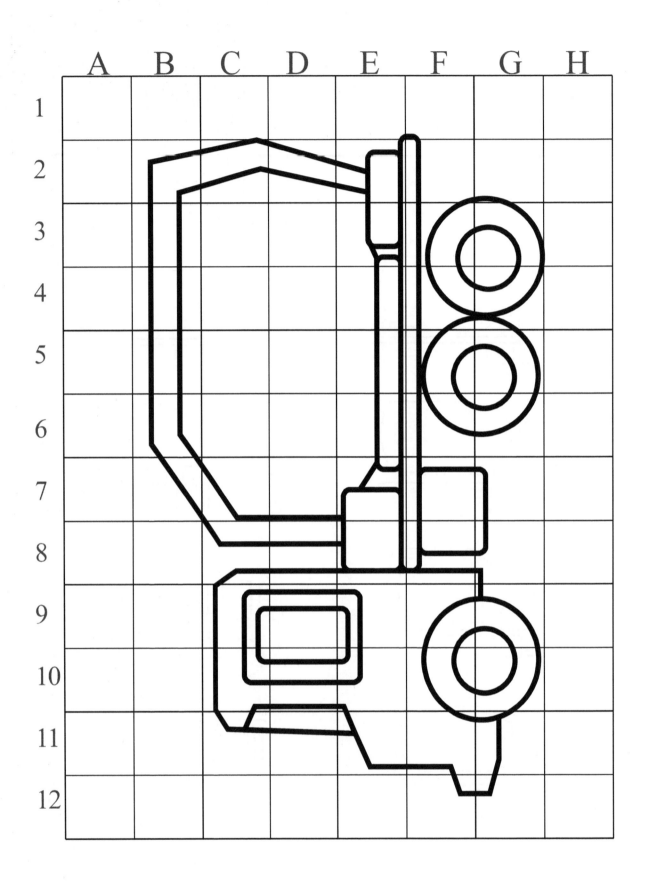

12. Your drawing may
have a basic shape that
you can attempt to outline
using your initial grid.

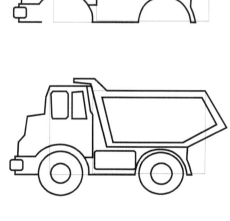

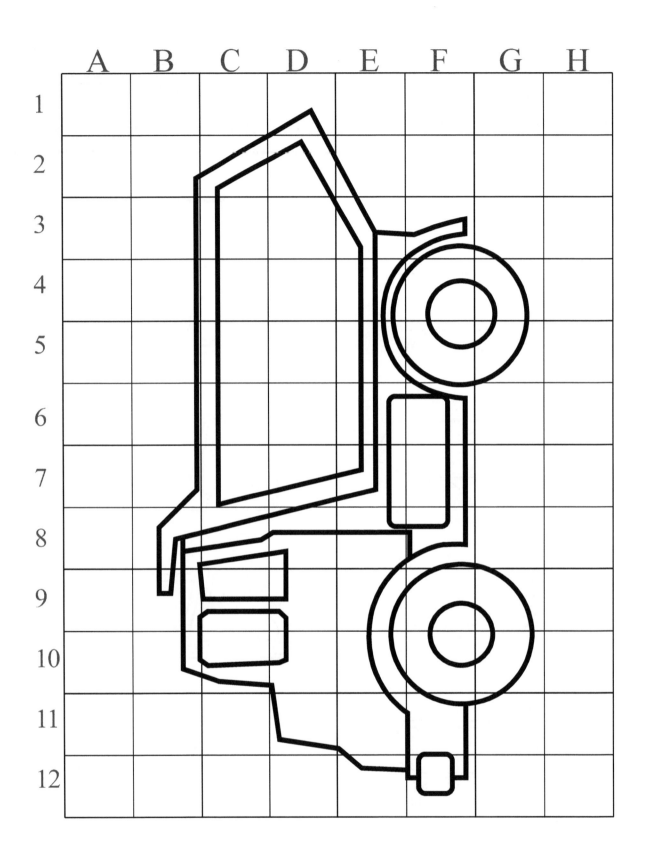

	A	B	C	D	E	F	G	H
1								
2								
3								
4								
5								
6								
7								
8								
9								
10								
11								
12								

13. More complex drawings require a lot more planning. One small step at time is the best approach to take, as all of those steps will add up.

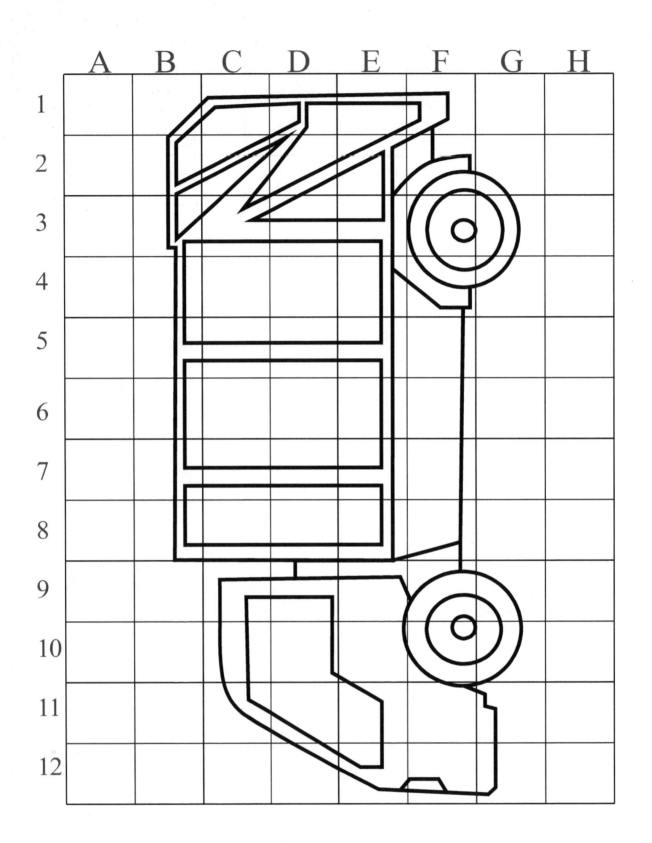

A B C D E F G H

1 2 3 4 5 6 7 8 9 10 11 12

15. It can be very difficult to get things right the first time, but remember the more you draw the better you will get at it.

1
2
3
4
5
6
7
8
9
10
11
12

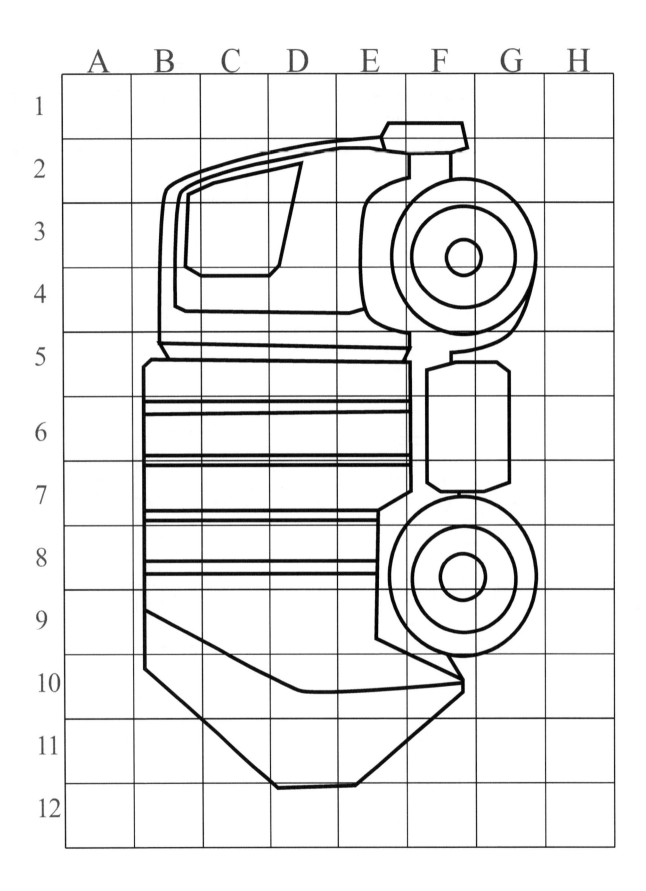

15. Try swapping part of your drawing with that of another from this book. This can lead to very interesting creations.

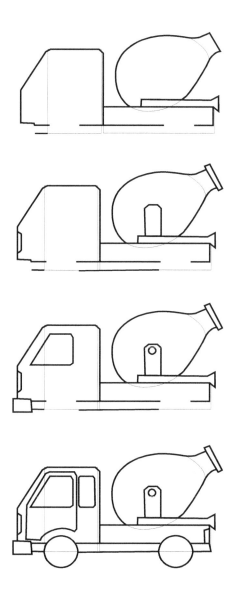

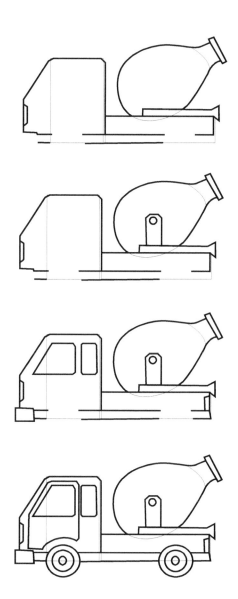

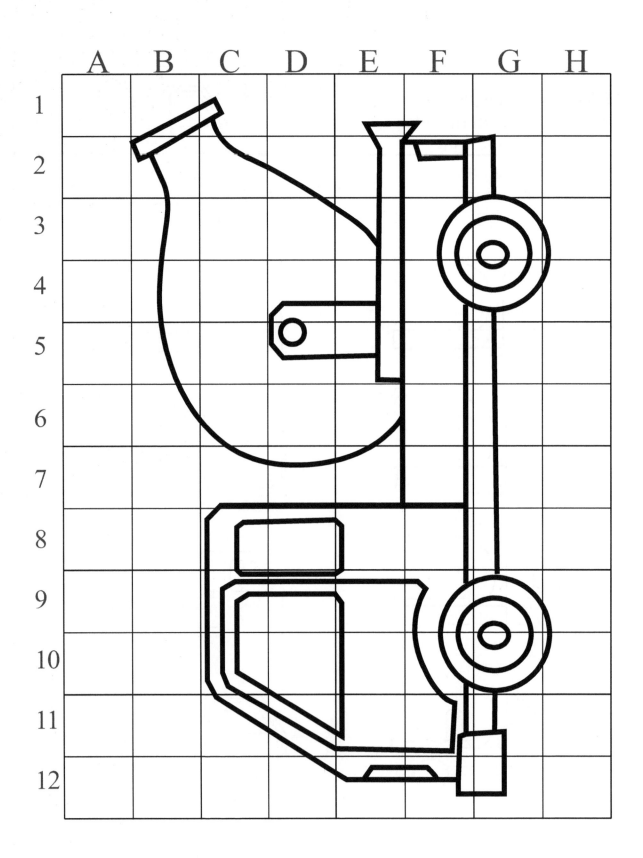

16. When you draw from a side view it is called a profile.

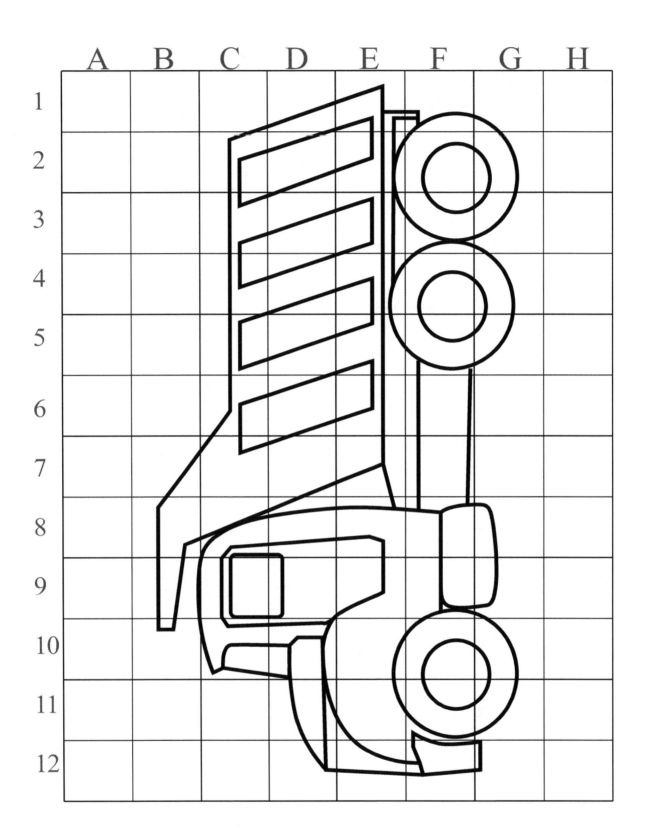

17. To become an expert at something you may need to spend thousands of hours doing it. Expert artists will often have spent more than 10,000 hours practising.

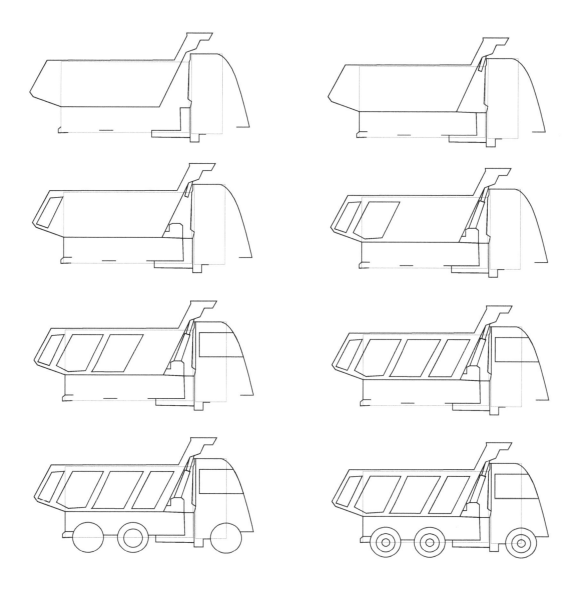

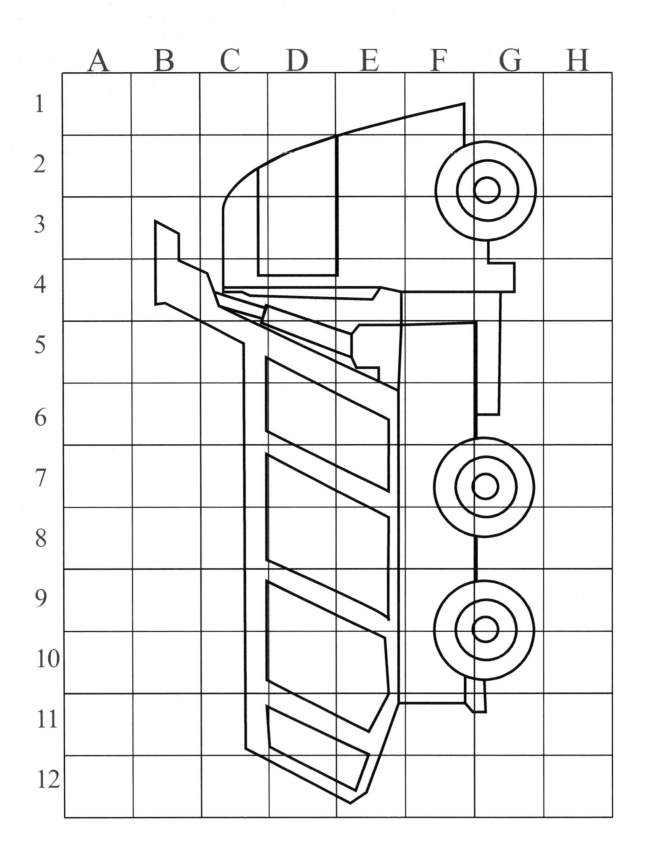

	A	B	C	D	E	F	G	H
1								
2								
3								
4								
5								
6								
7								
8								
9								
10								
11								
12								

18. We all make mistakes, even the most successful people in life do. What sets successful people apart is how they respond to their mistakes.

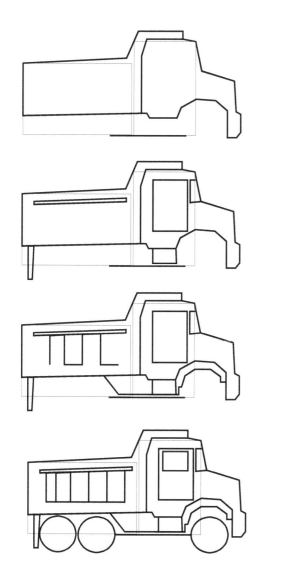

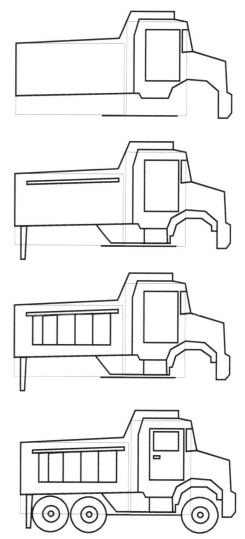

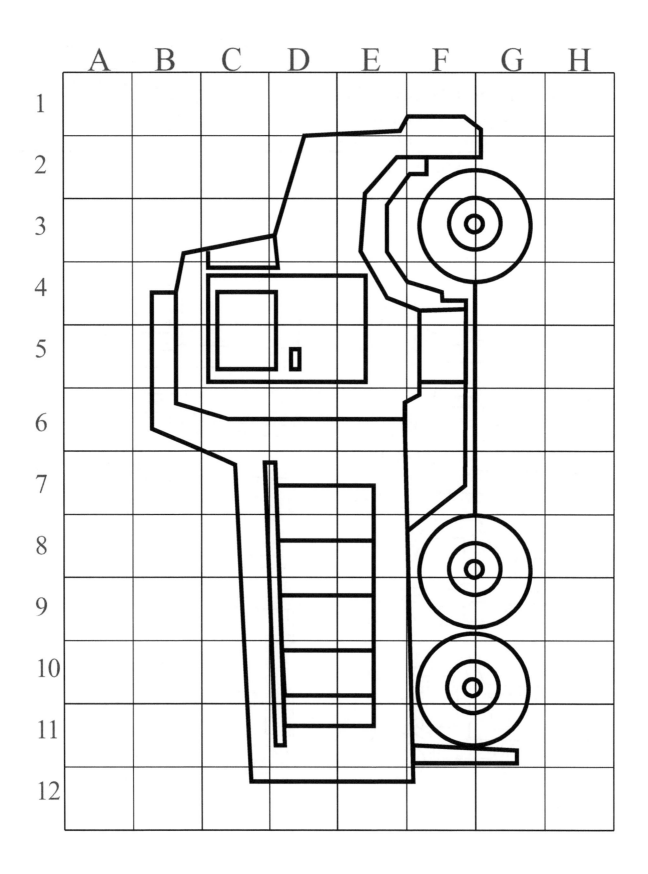

19. For larger projects focus on one step at a time. People have walked thousands of miles by taking one step at a time.

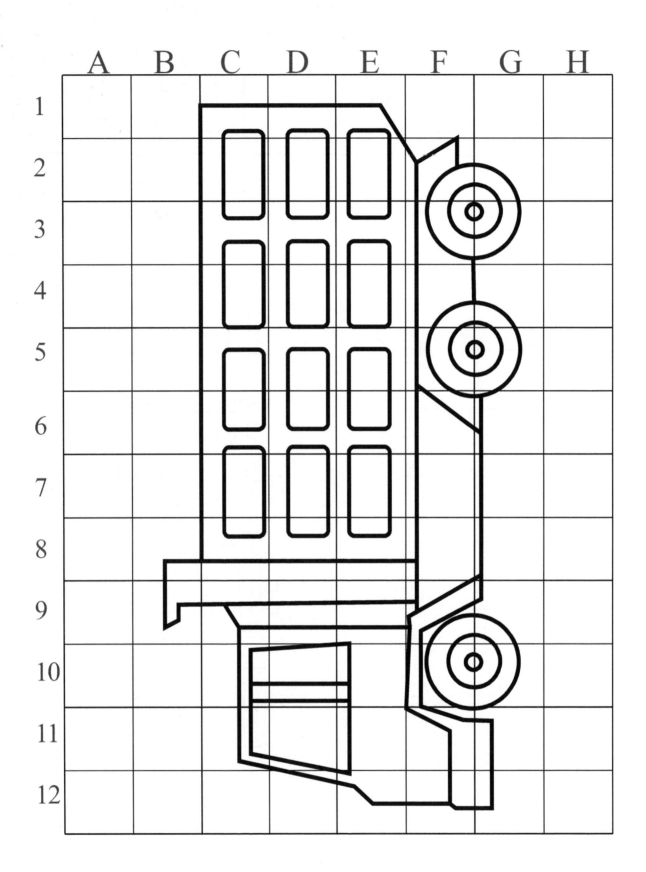

20. If you are struggling for ideas for your work, take a break and do something different. Your mind will keep working in the background for you. Some of our greatest ideas come to us while we sleep.

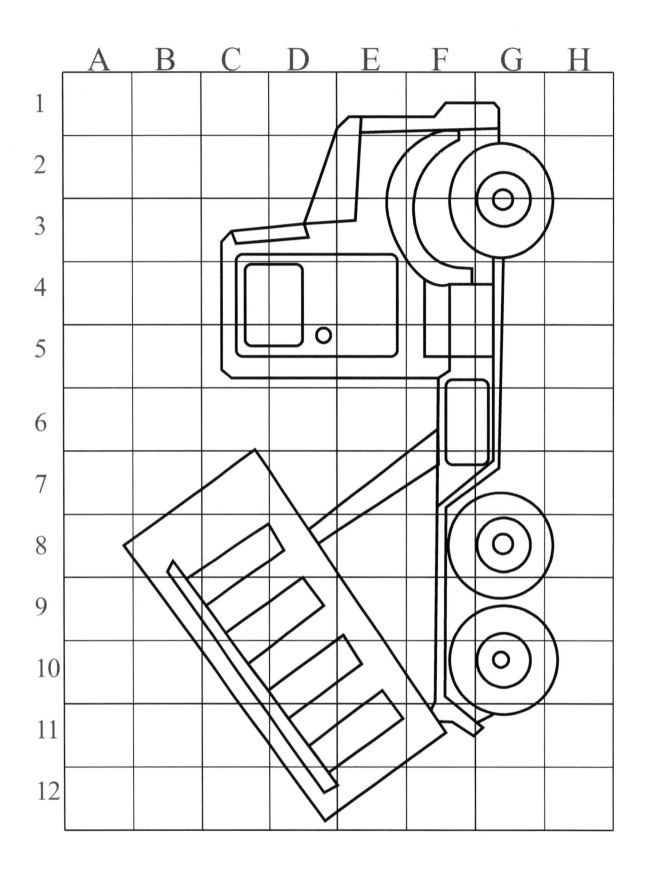

21. If you find that you are rushing, stop what you are doing and take a break. Rushing too much will reduce the quality of your work.

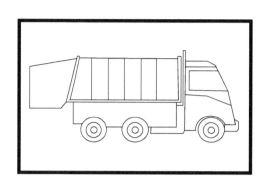

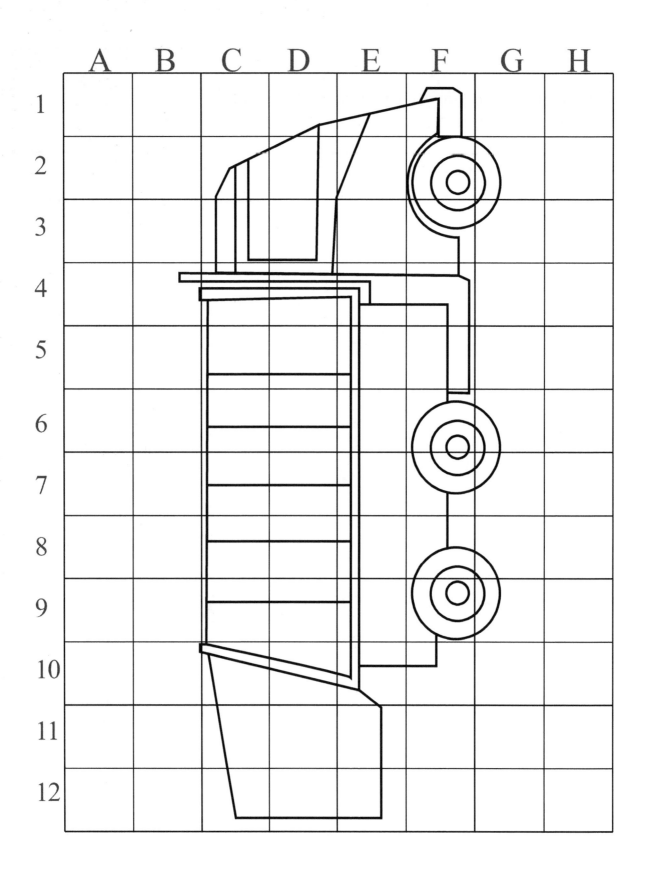

22. If a project looks too difficult to complete all in one go, complete part of it and come back to it a little later. It will then feel less overwhelming.

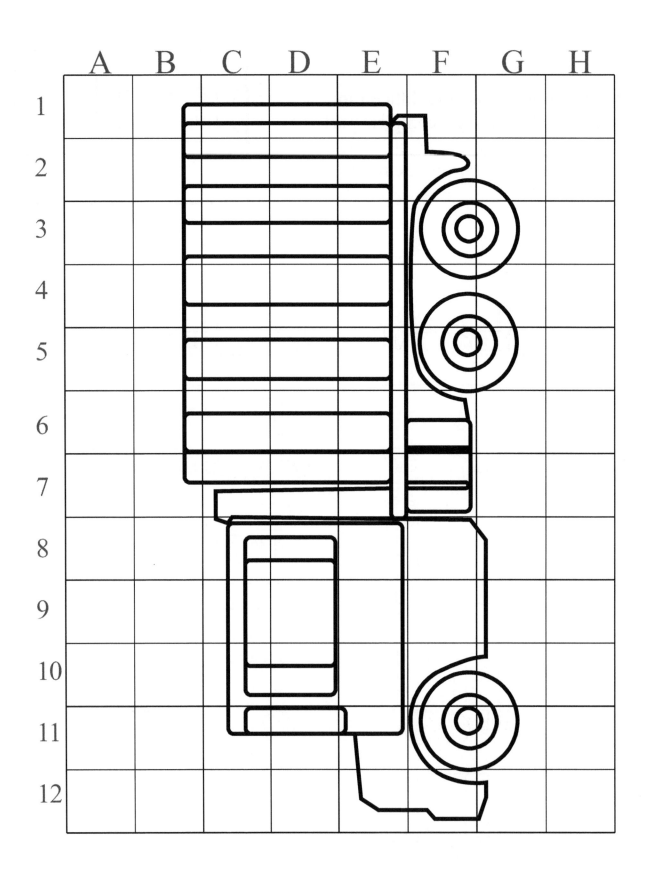

23. It is very rare to see drawings that are exactly alike. It is usually small details that separate them.

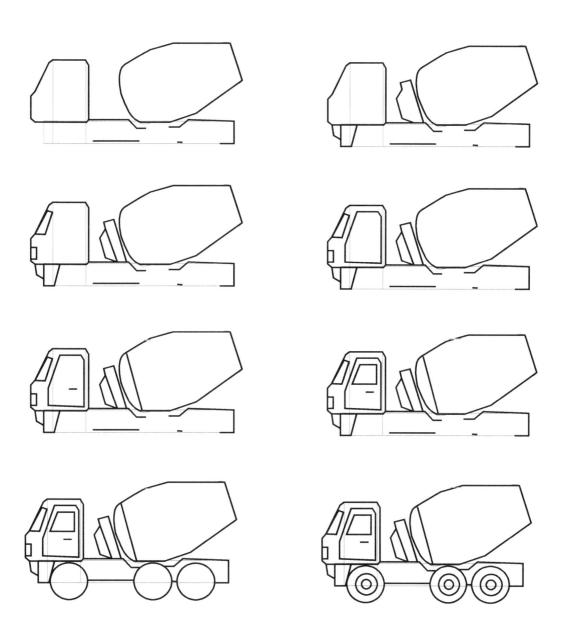

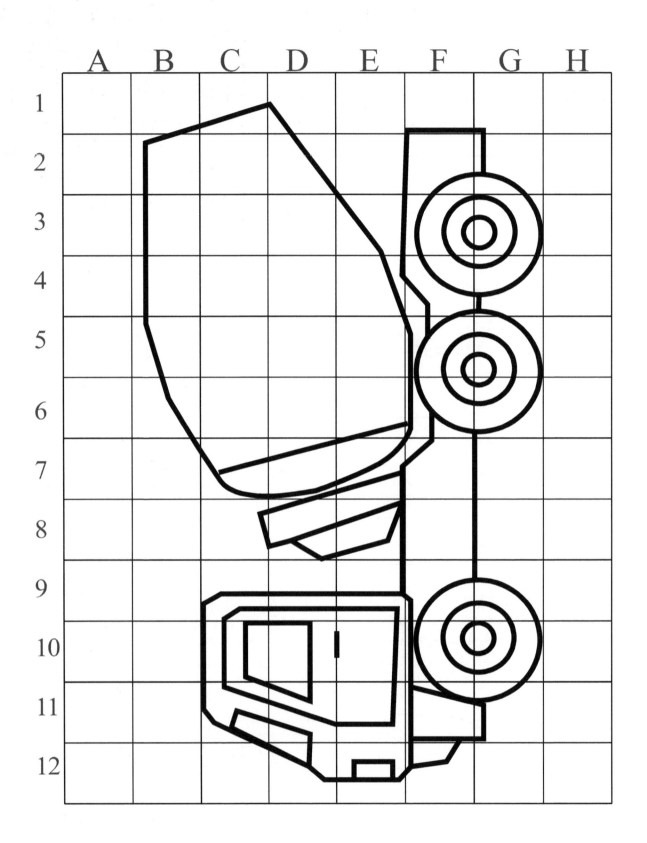

24. To create a mirror image draw everything the opposite way.

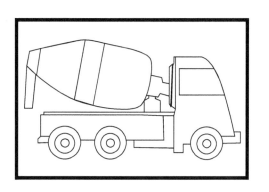

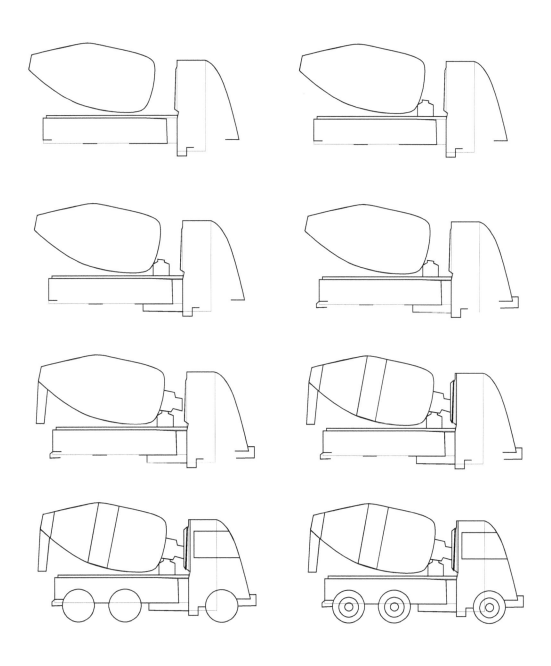

53

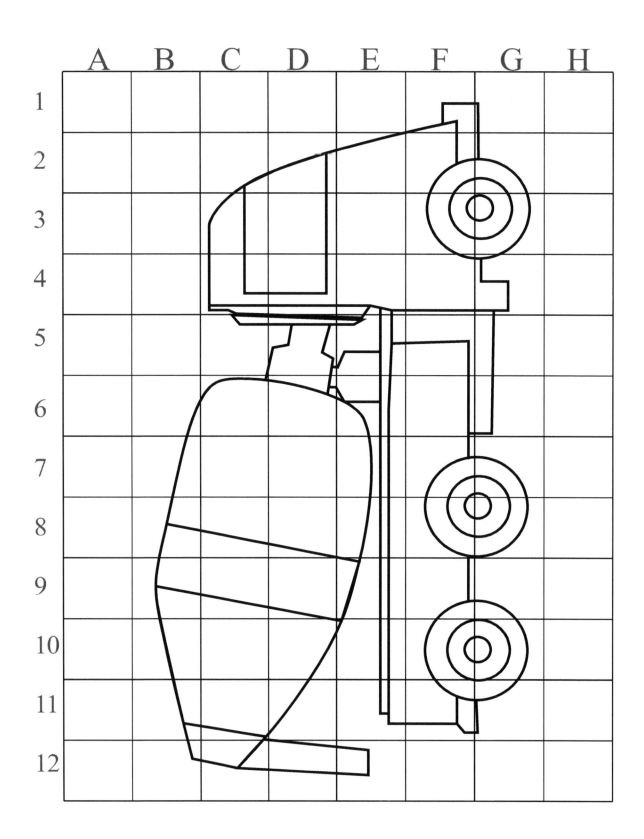

25. Try lengthening parts
of your drawing to see
what effect it gives.

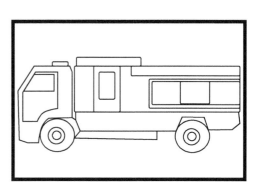

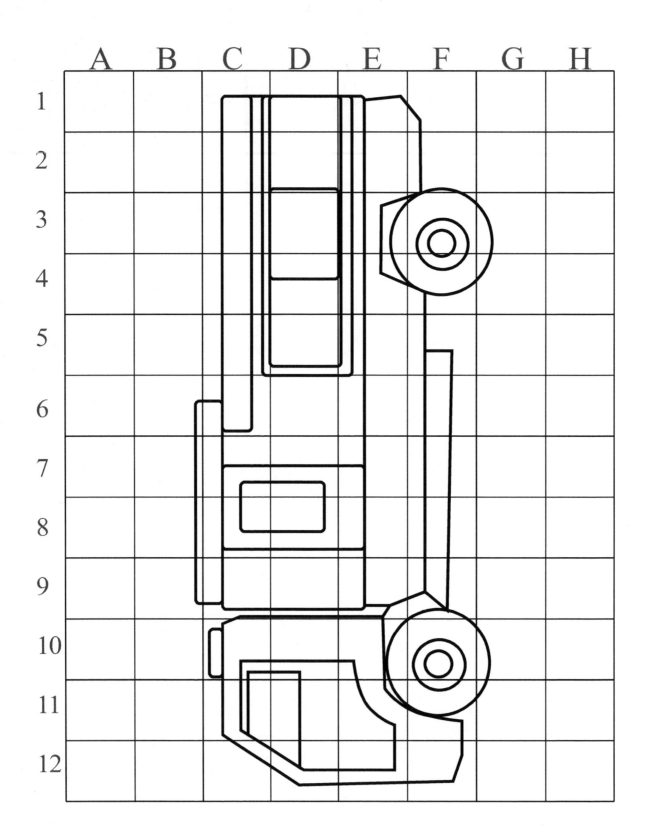

26. Adding one section of your project at a time will make your drawing feel less overwhelming.

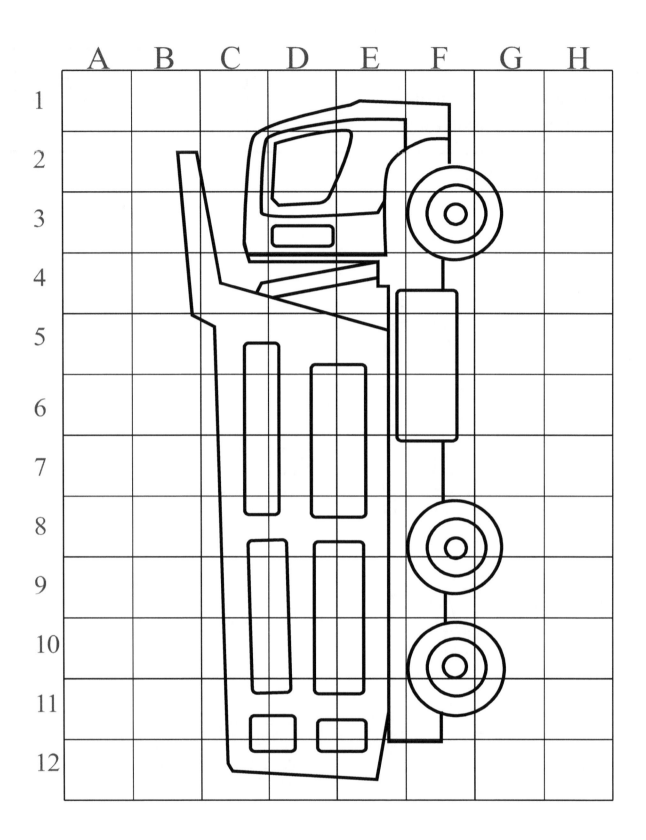

27. A basic grid will help you to easily organise your drawing.

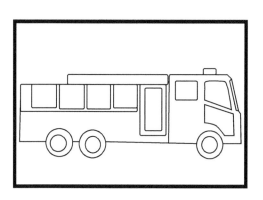

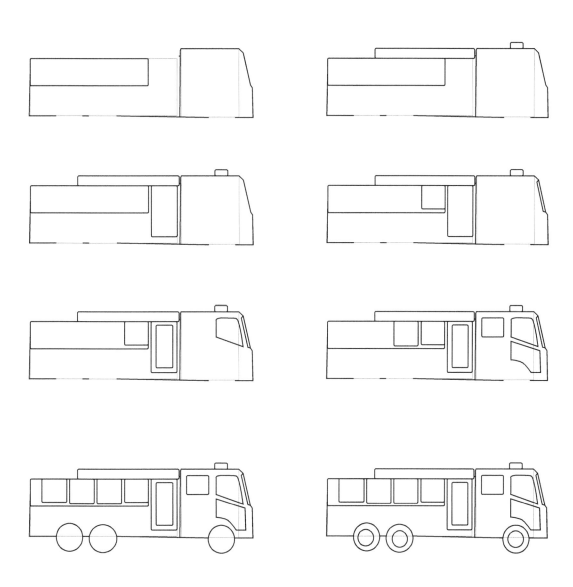

	A	B	C	D	E	F	G	H

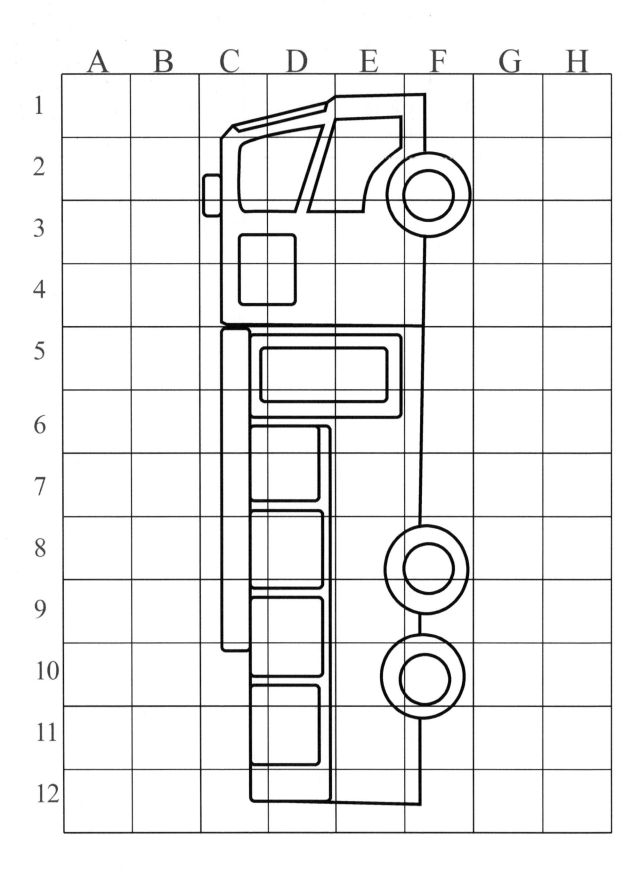

28. Add extra features to
your drawing to make it
look more original.

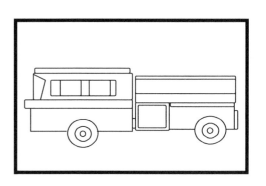

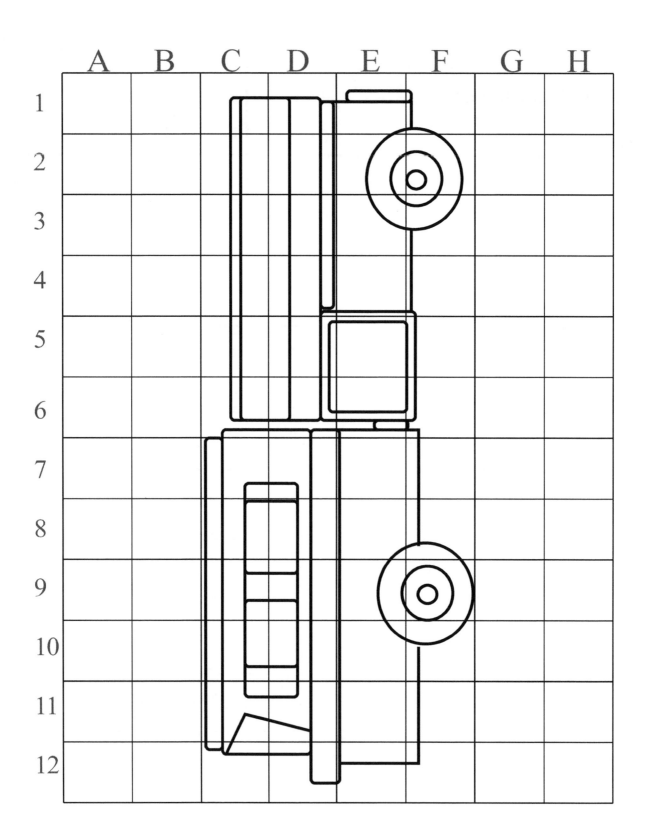

29. Ask questions to stimulate your creativity. Following this, listen to the suggestions your mind comes up with.

	A	B	C	D	E	F	G	H
1								
2								
3								
4								
5								
6								
7								
8								
9								
10								
11								
12								

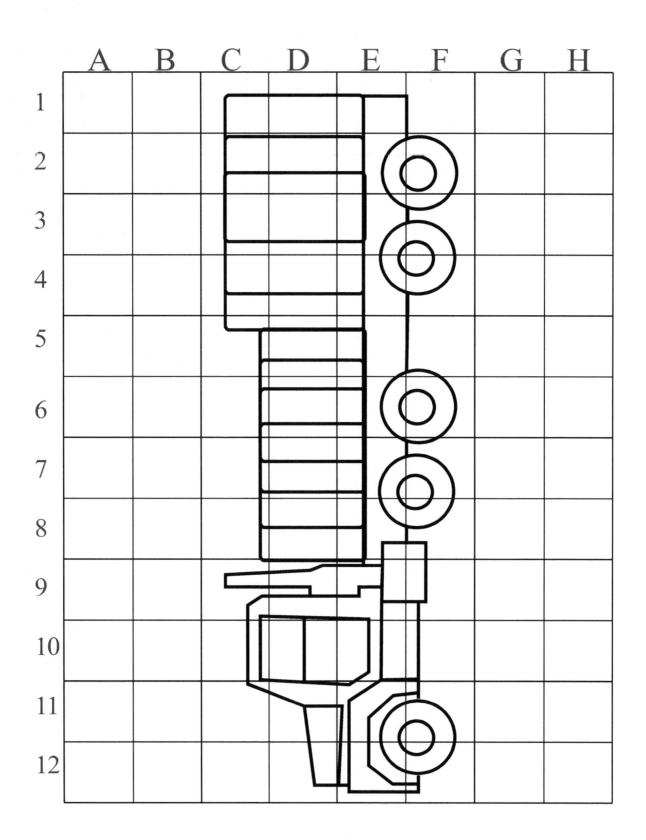

30. Your drawing may
have a basic shape that
you can attempt to outline
using your initial grid.

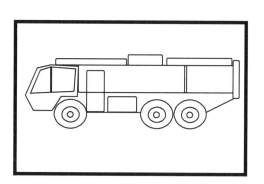

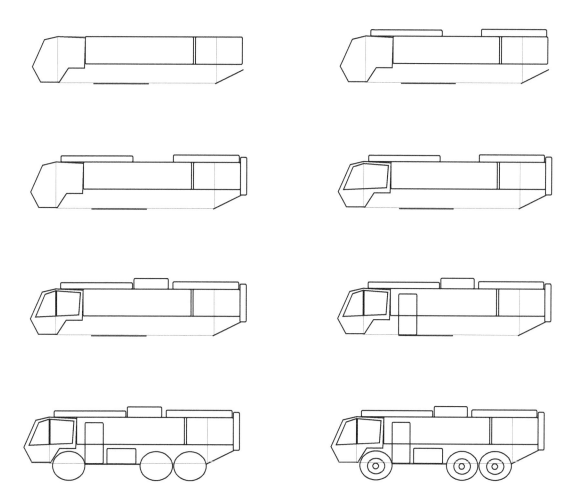

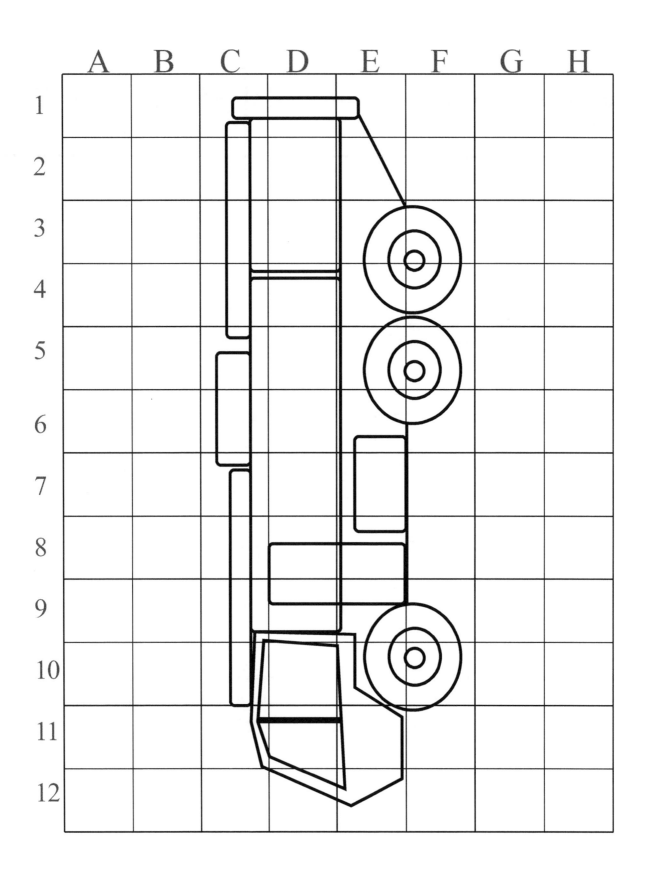

31. Try adjusting the angle
of your drawing.

	A	B	C	D	E	F	G	H

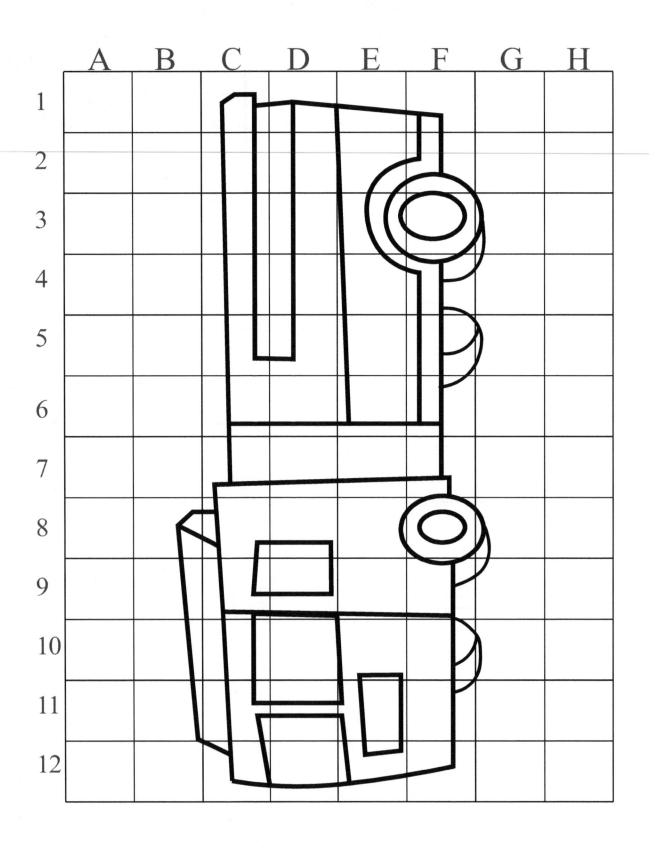

32. The angle of observation will mean alterations in your drawing.

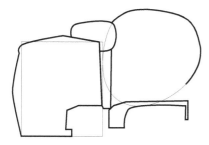
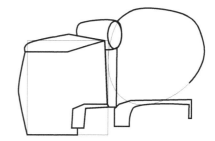

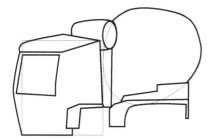
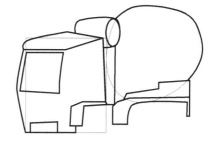

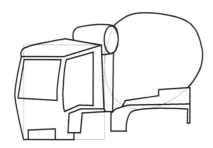

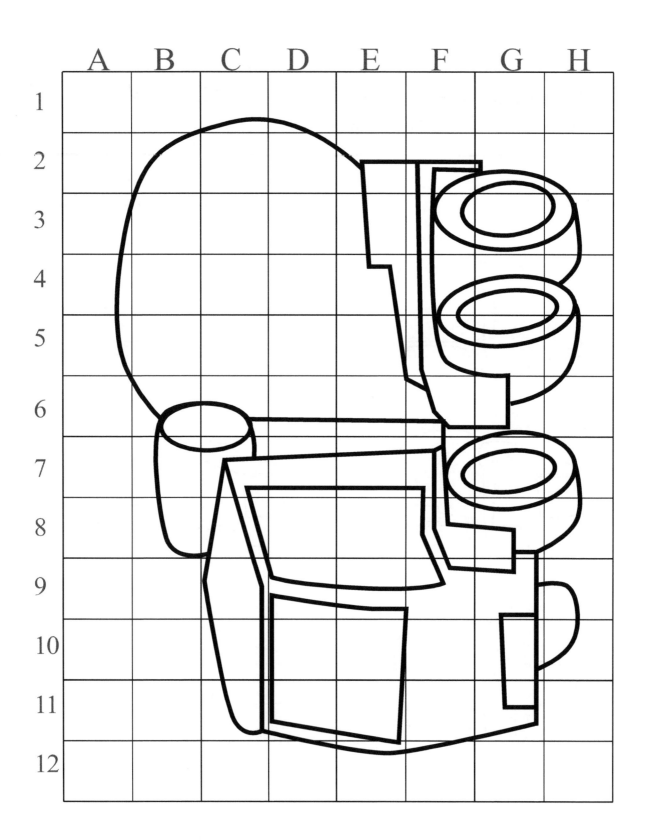

33. Here is another drawing
showing observation from an angle.

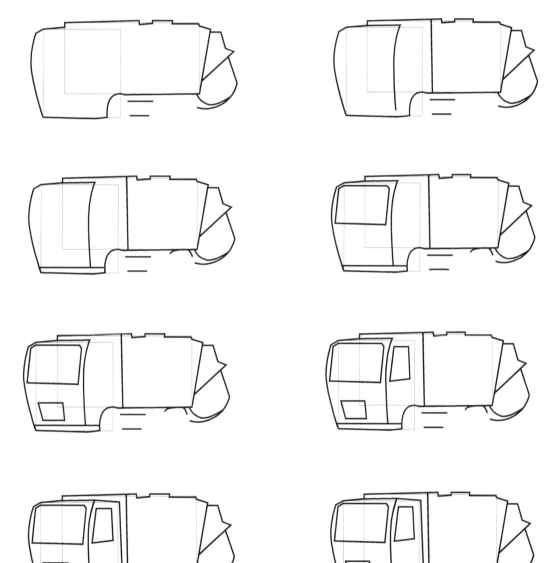

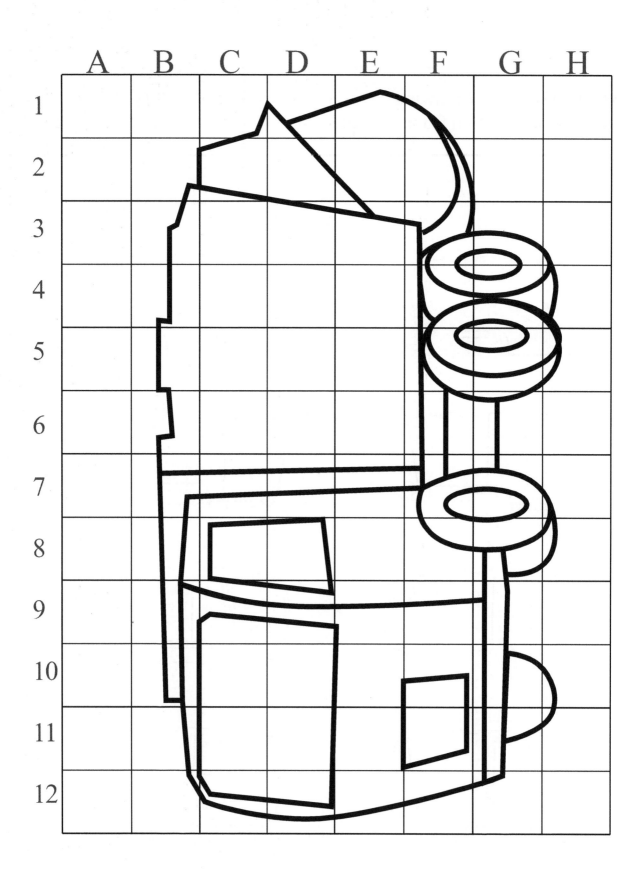

34. Drawing is a process of construction. Add one small part at a time.

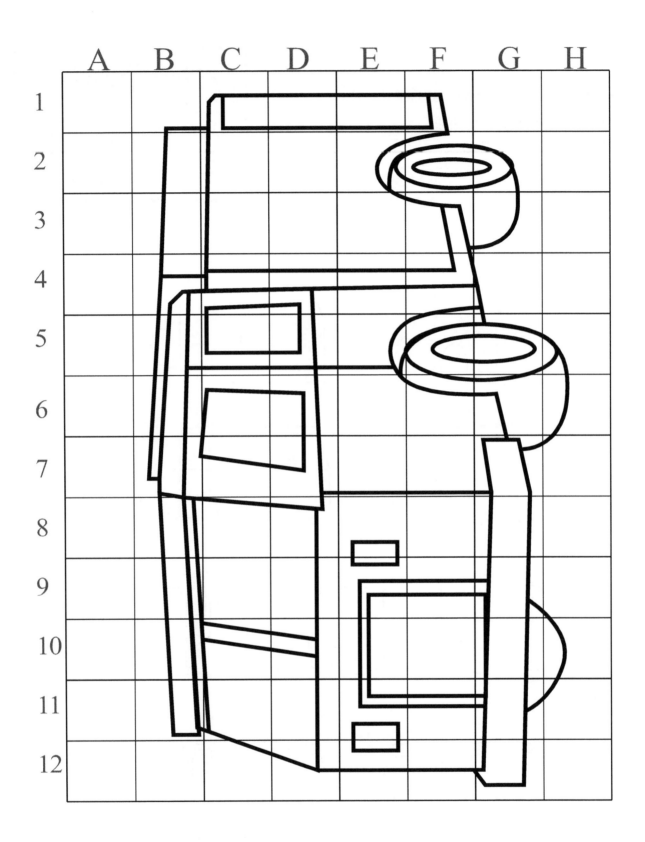

35. The eyes are designed to see things in three dimensions. The brain of the observer will often alter information to make it fit. This is how optical illusions occur.

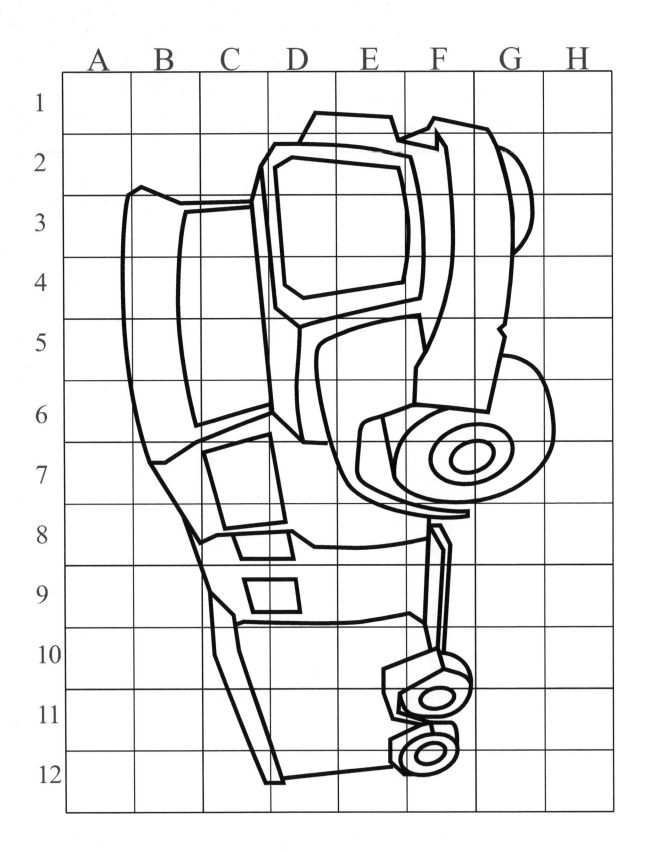

36. You can create 3D type effects by enlarging some parts and making other parts smaller.

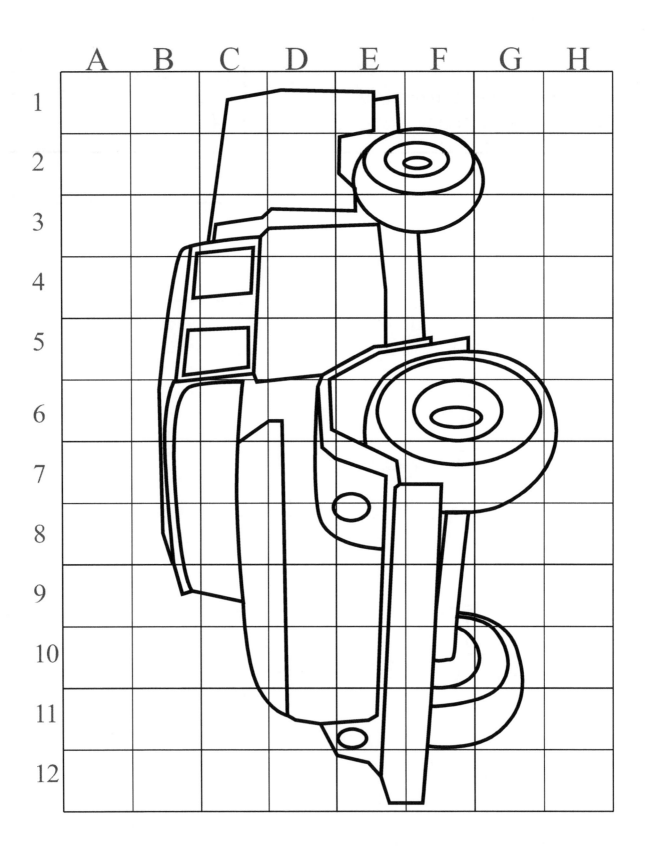

37. Here is another
example of a 3D effect.

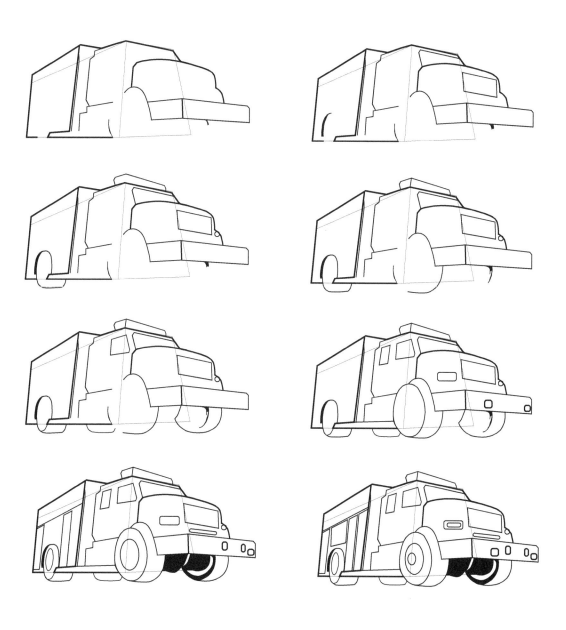

	A	B	C	D	E	F	G	H
1								
2								
3								
4								
5								
6								
7								
8								
9								
10								
11								
12								

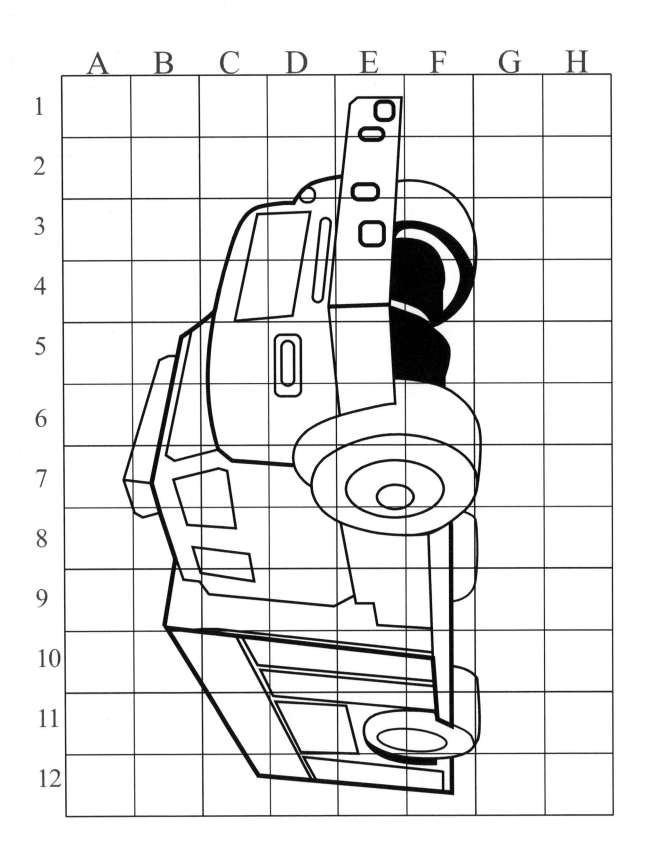

38. Here I have created a perspective from above.

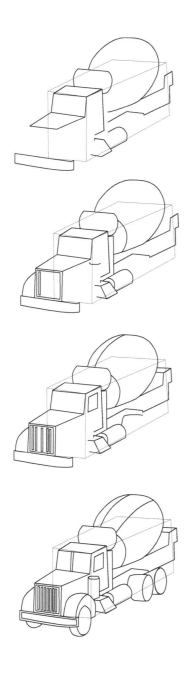

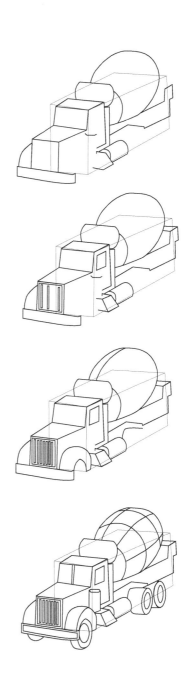

	A	B	C	D	E	F	G	H

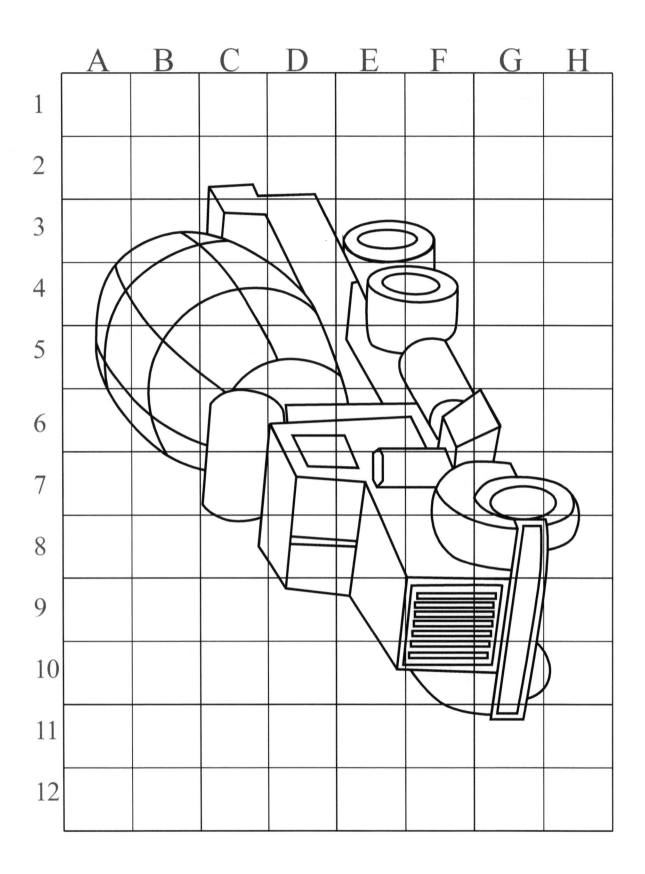

39. Taking photographs from different angles can often help with laying out the proportions of a figure or an object.

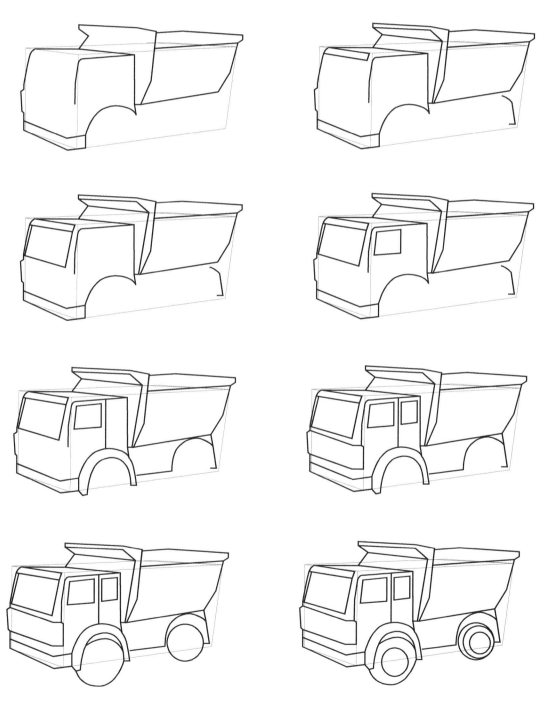

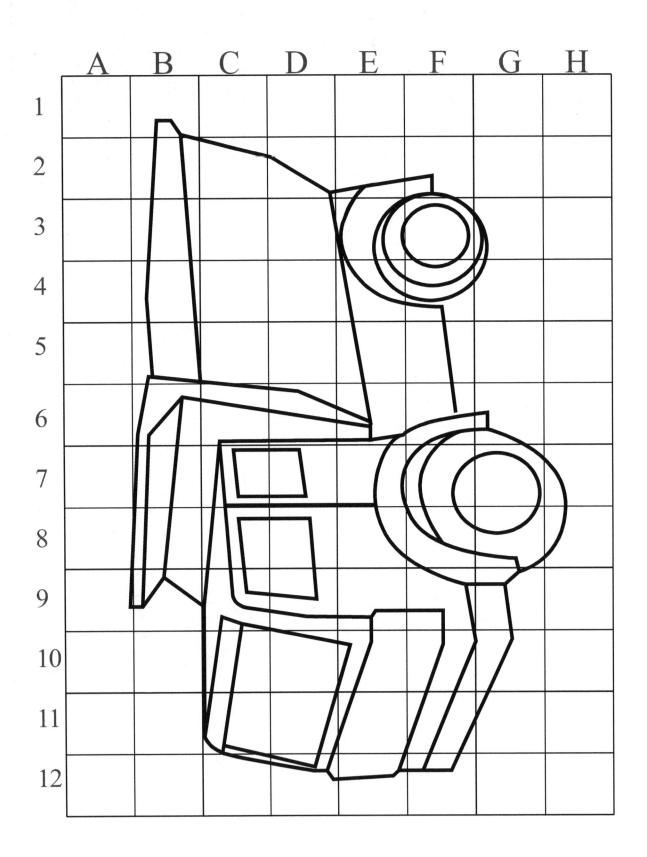

CPSIA information can be obtained
at www.ICGtesting.com
Printed in the USA
BVHW011006030122
625349BV00016B/449